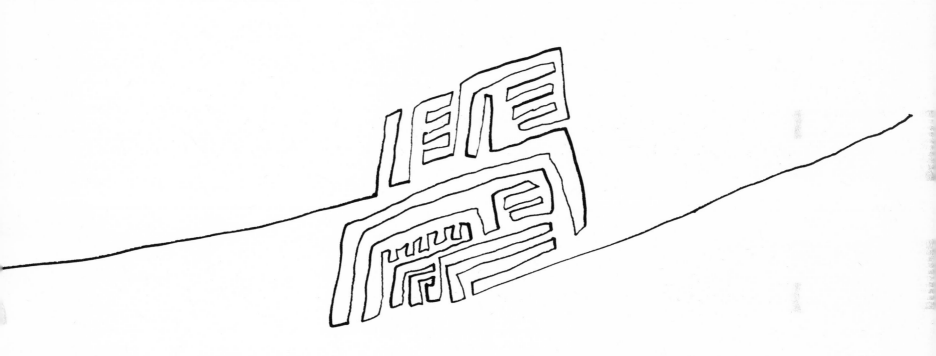

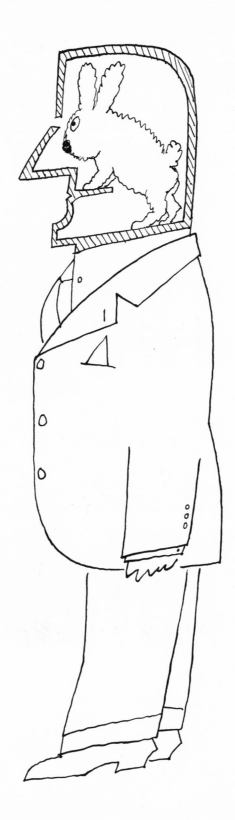

STEINBERG

THE LABYRINTH

HARPER & BROTHERS, PUBLISHERS, NEW YORK

Books by Saul Steinberg

ALL IN LINE (1945)

THE ART OF LIVING (1949)

THE PASSPORT (1954)

THE LABYRINTH (1960)

Of the 341 drawings in this book, 153 originally appeared in *The New Yorker*;
6 in *Harper's Magazine*; 3 in *Life*; 2 in *New World Writing*; 2 in *Britannica Book of the
Year, 1957-58*; 1 in *Scientific American*; 8 in *Femina-Illustration*; 2 in *L'Express*;
and 5 in *Encounter*.

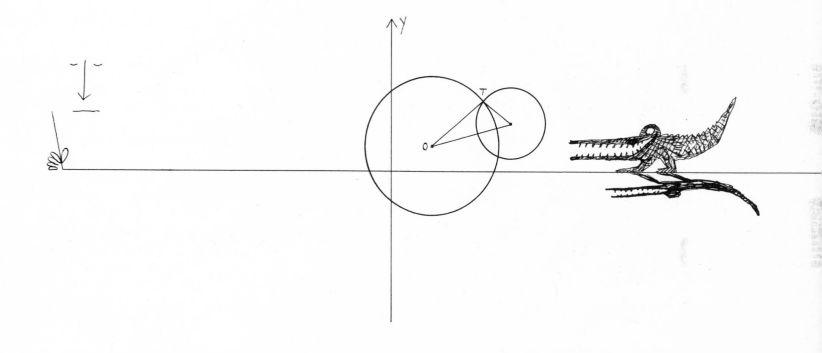

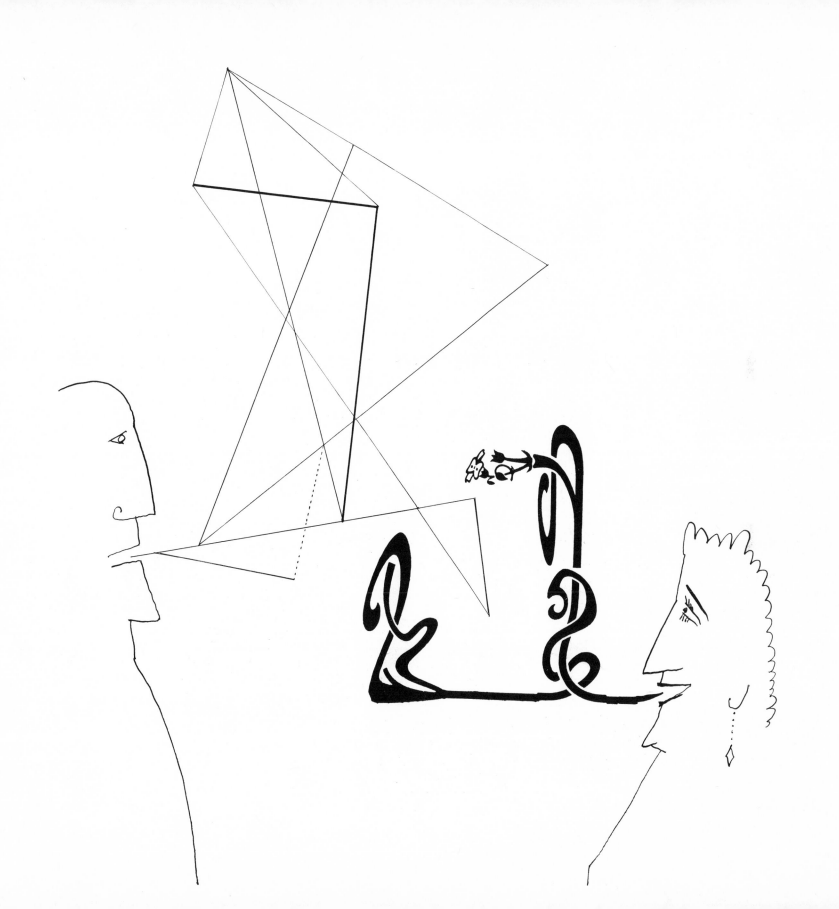

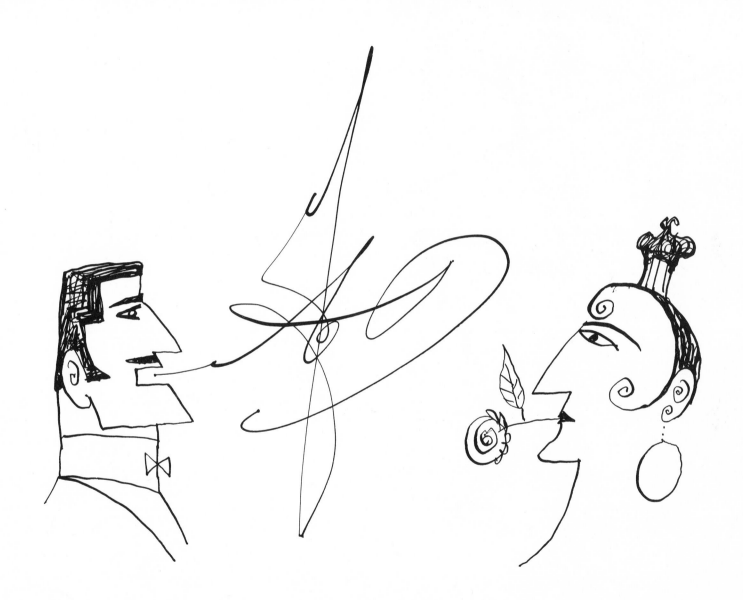

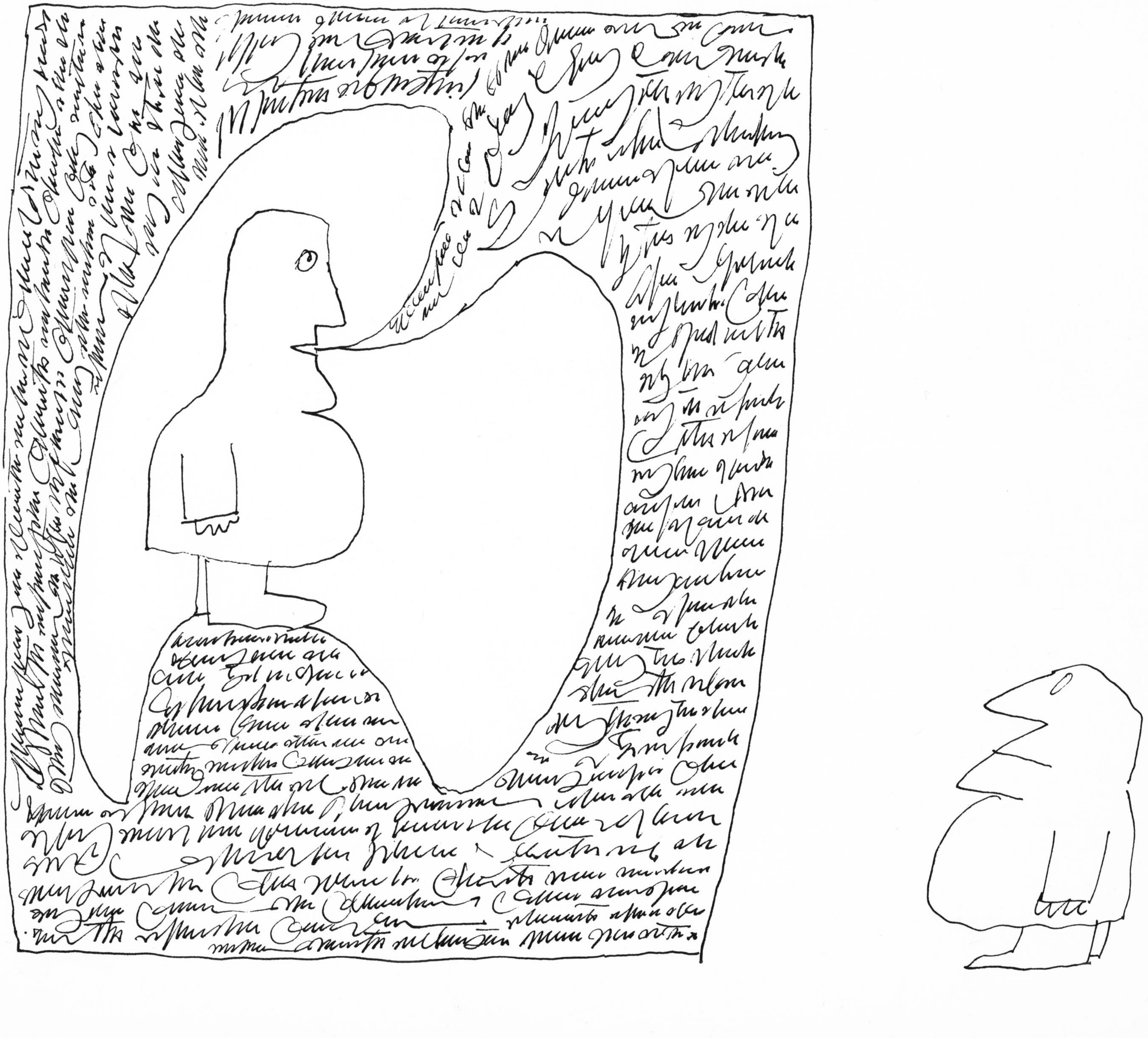

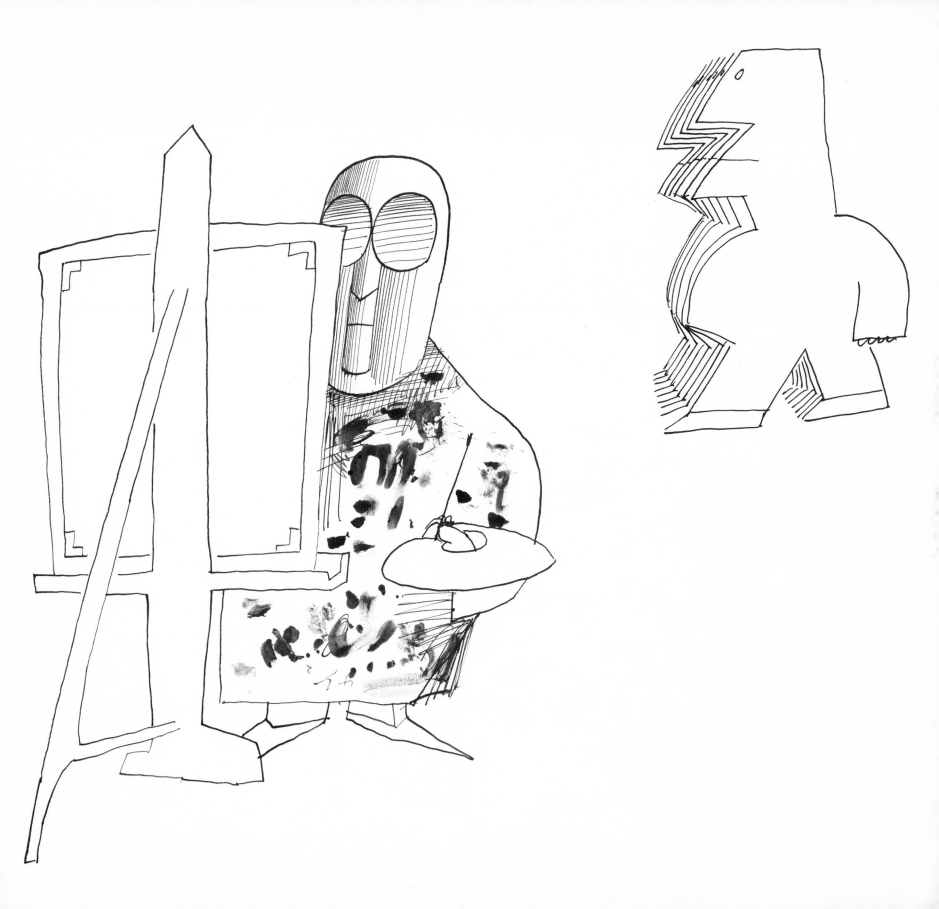

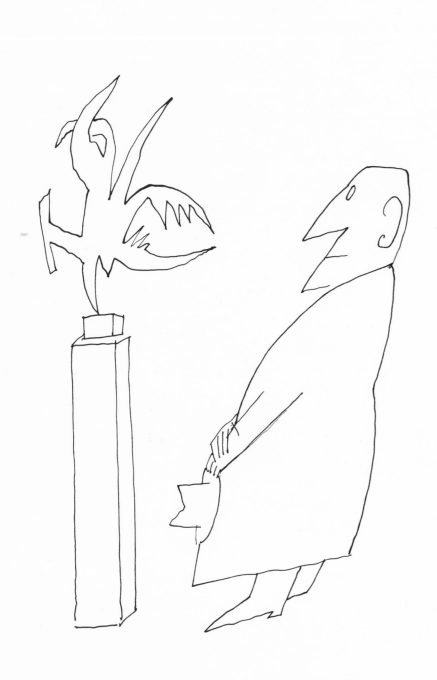

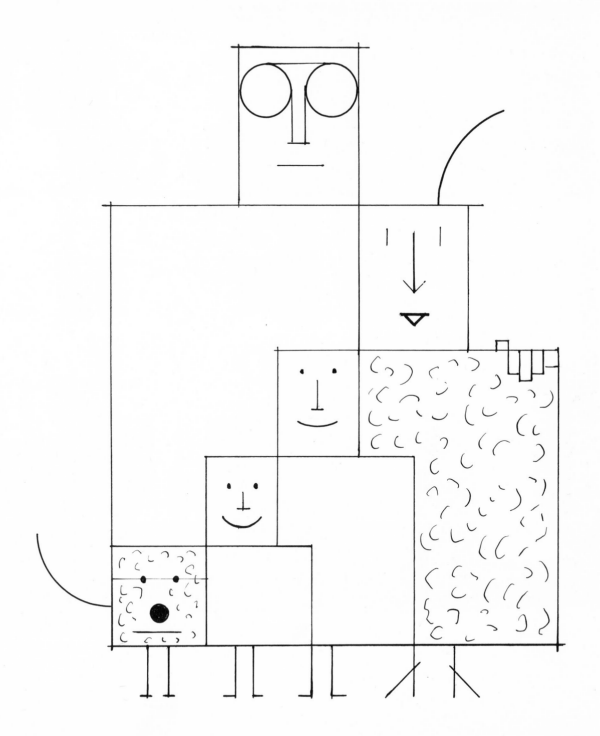

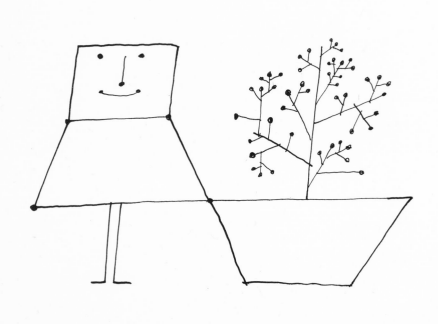

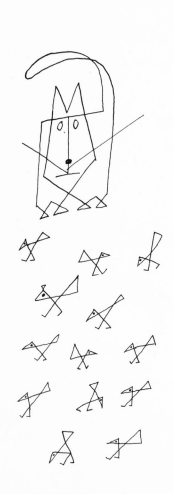
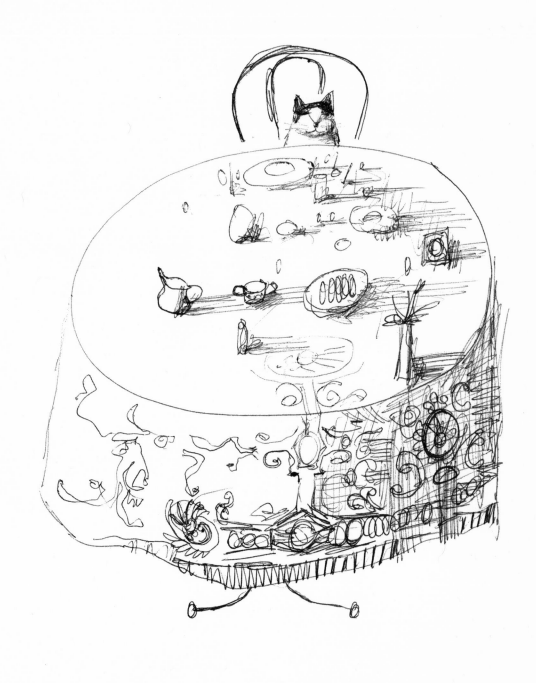

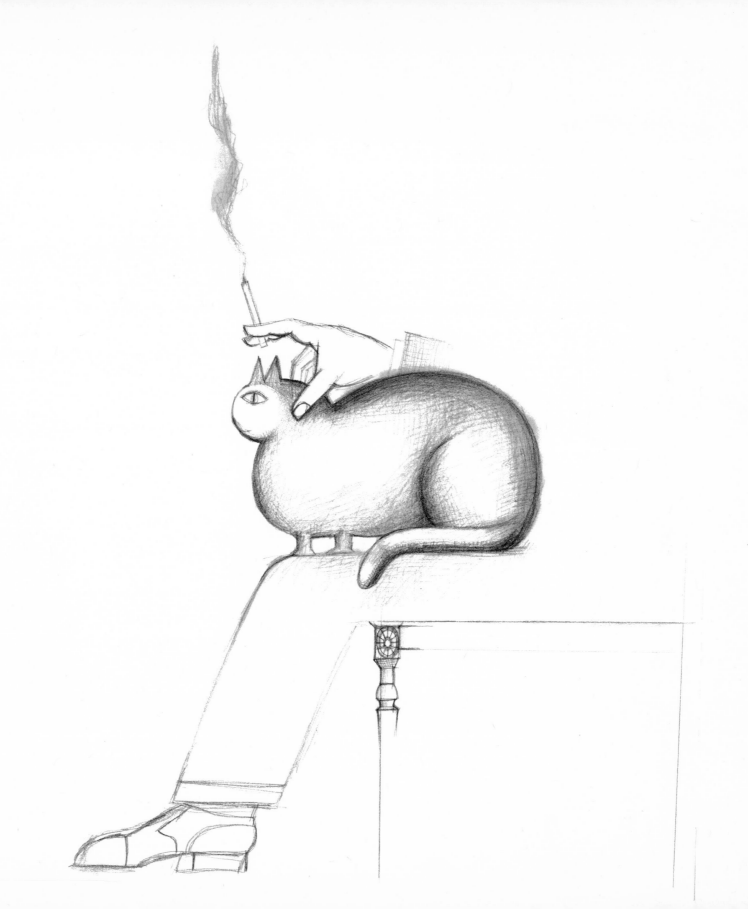

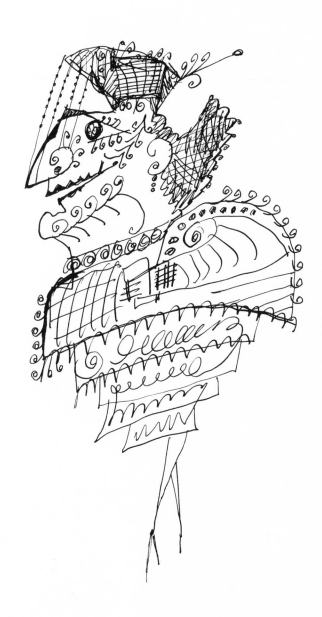

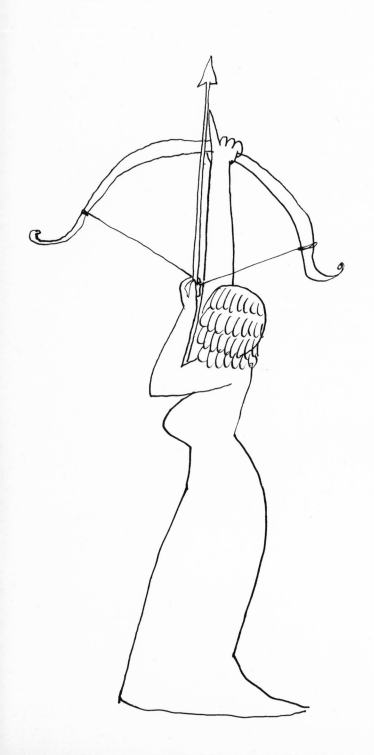

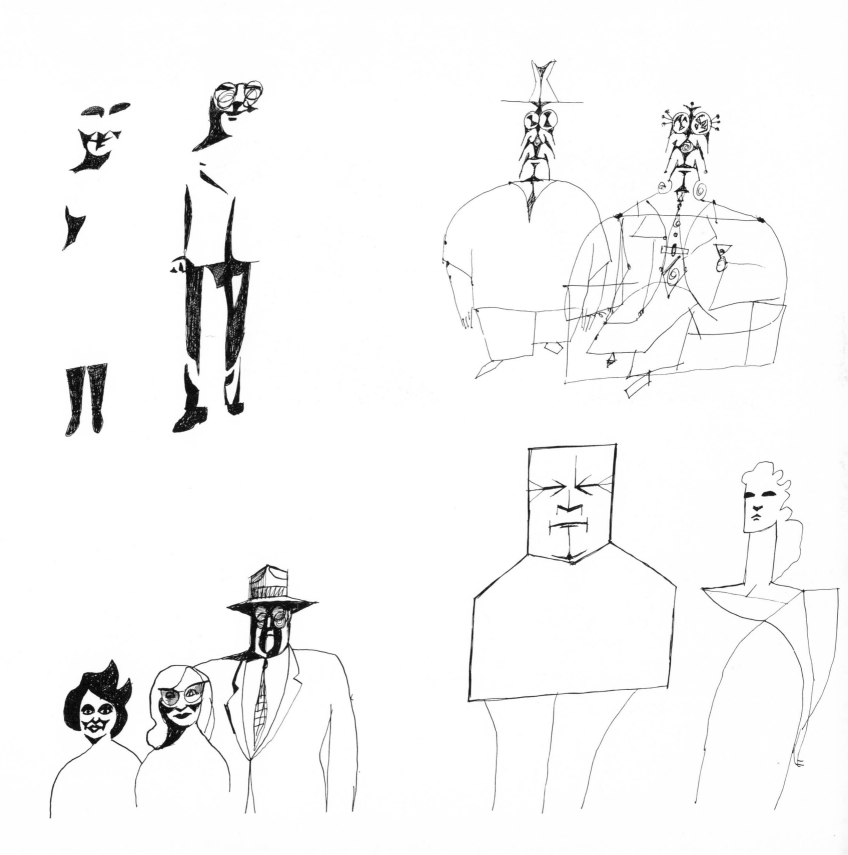

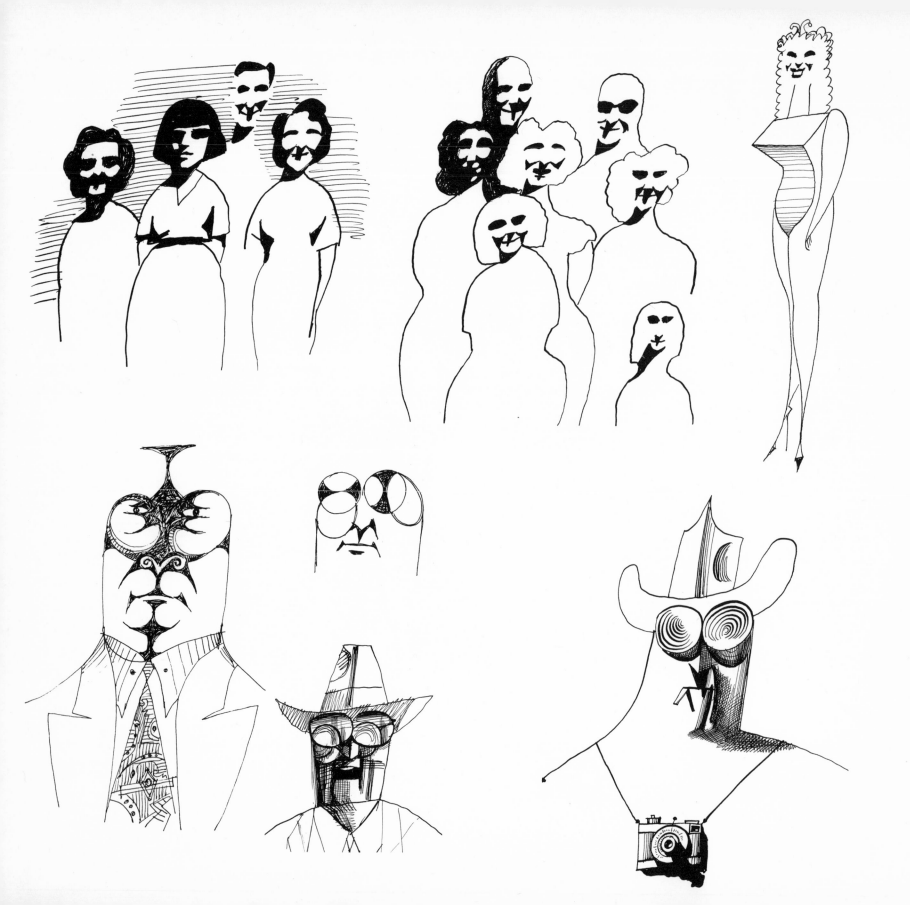

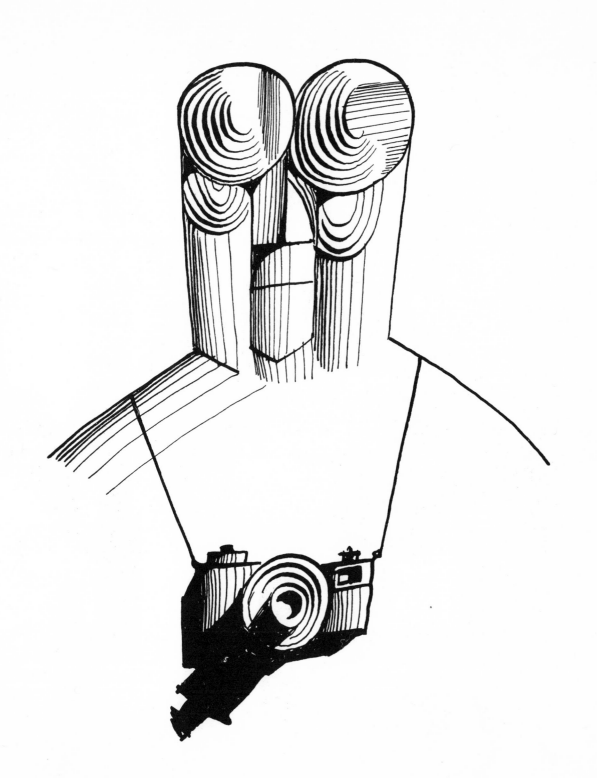

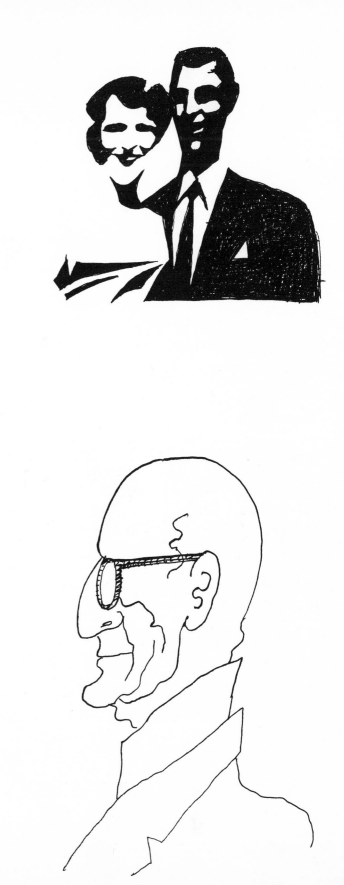

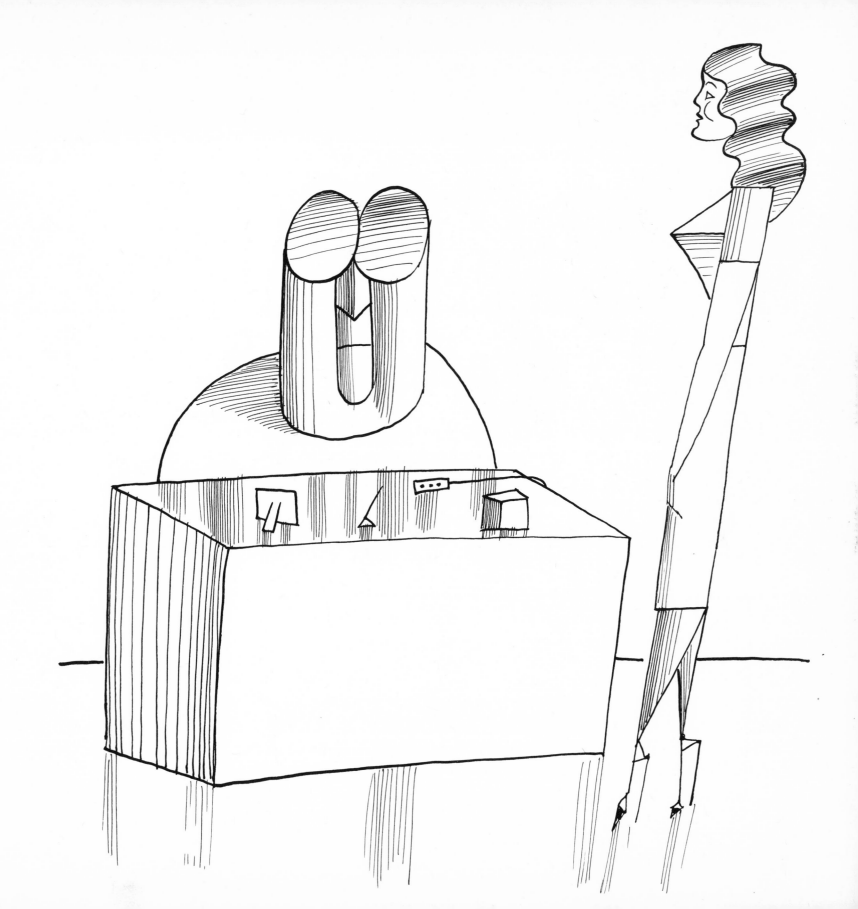

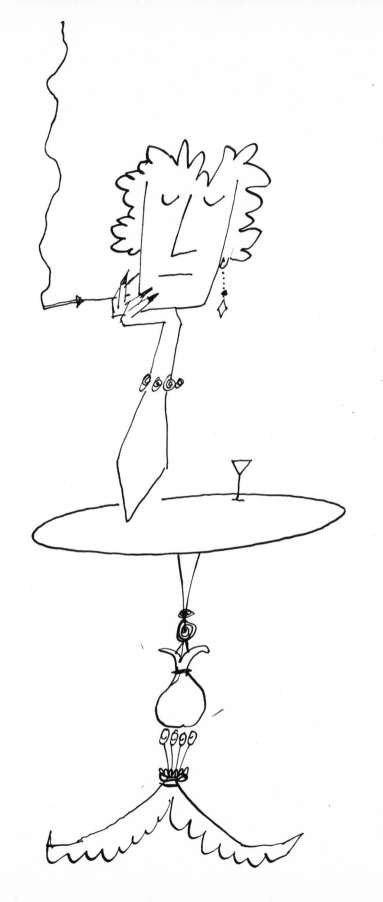

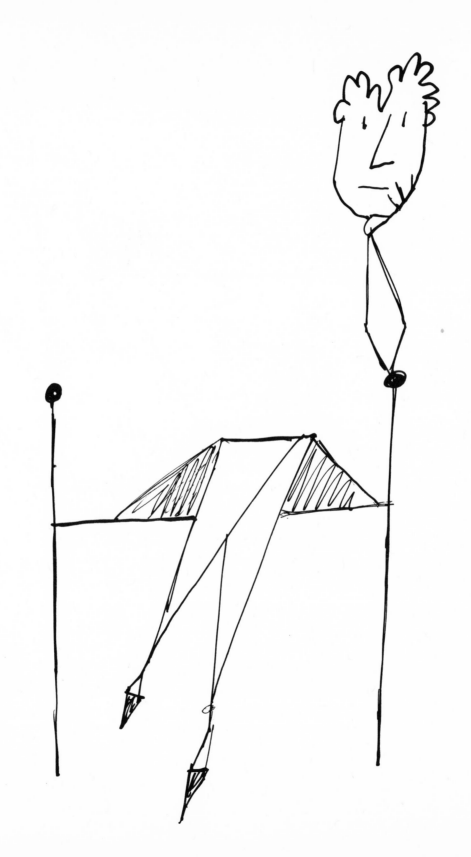

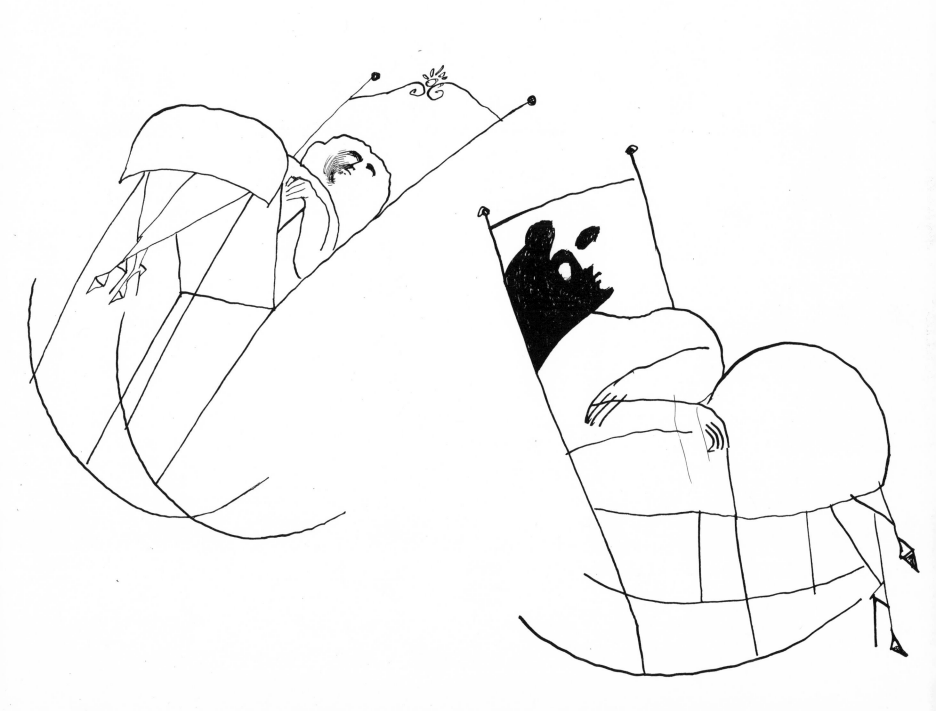

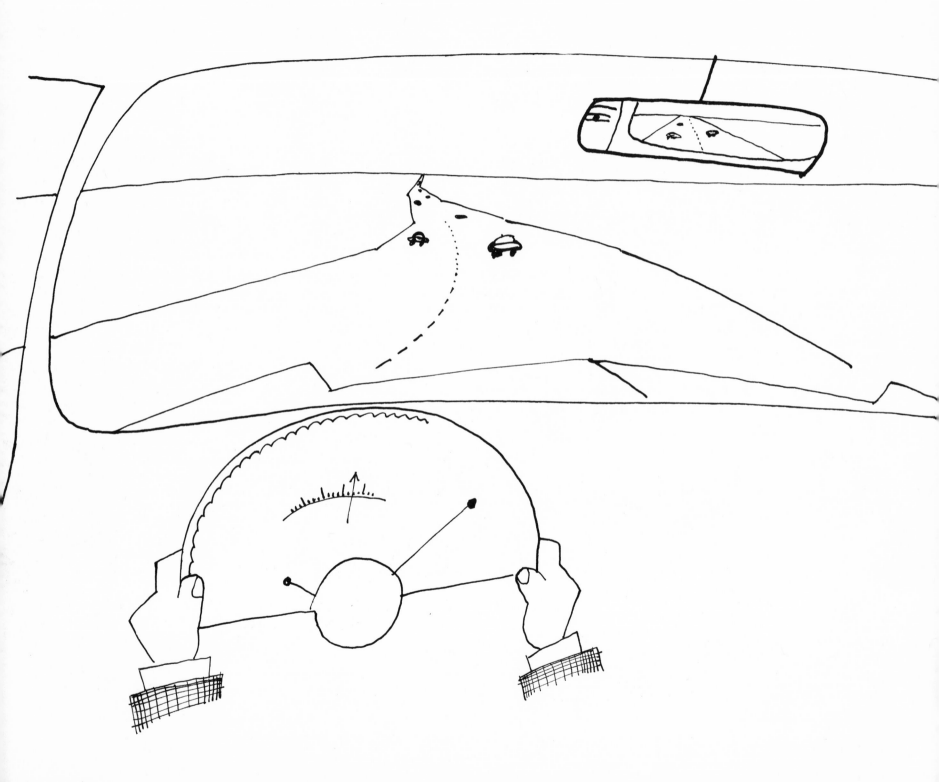

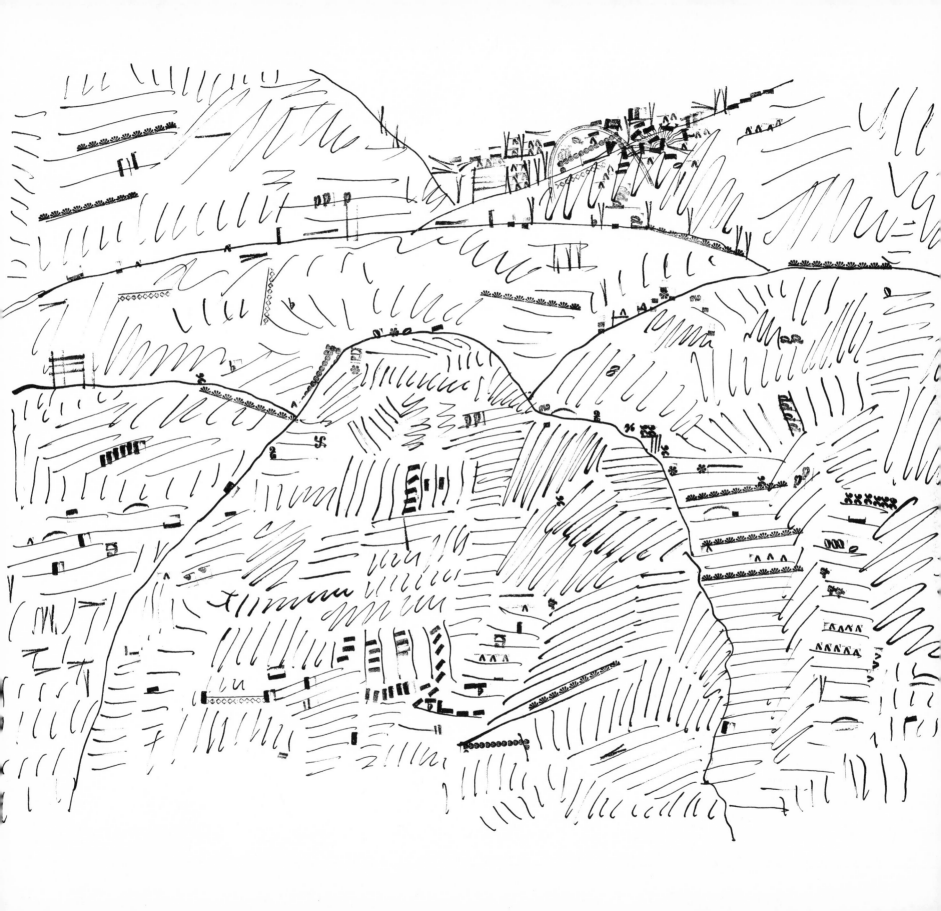

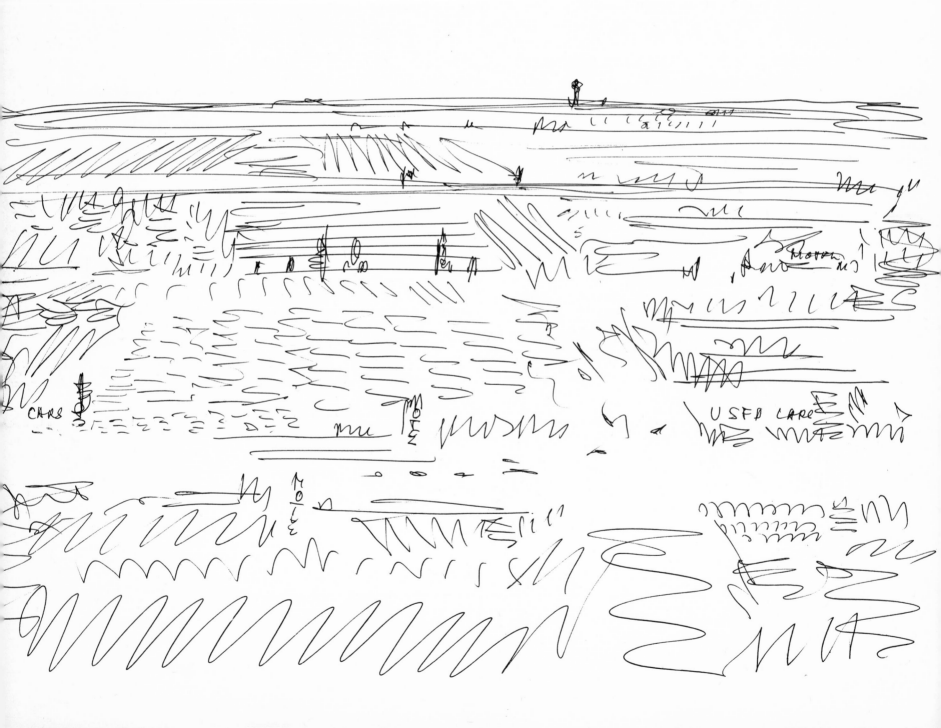

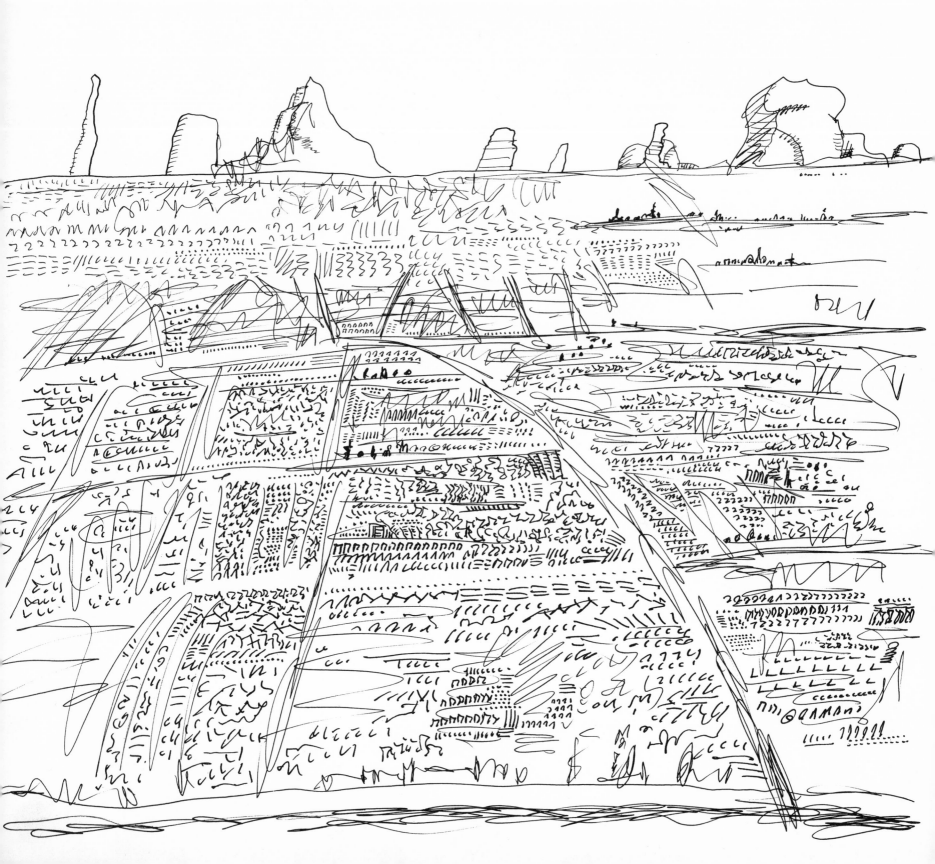

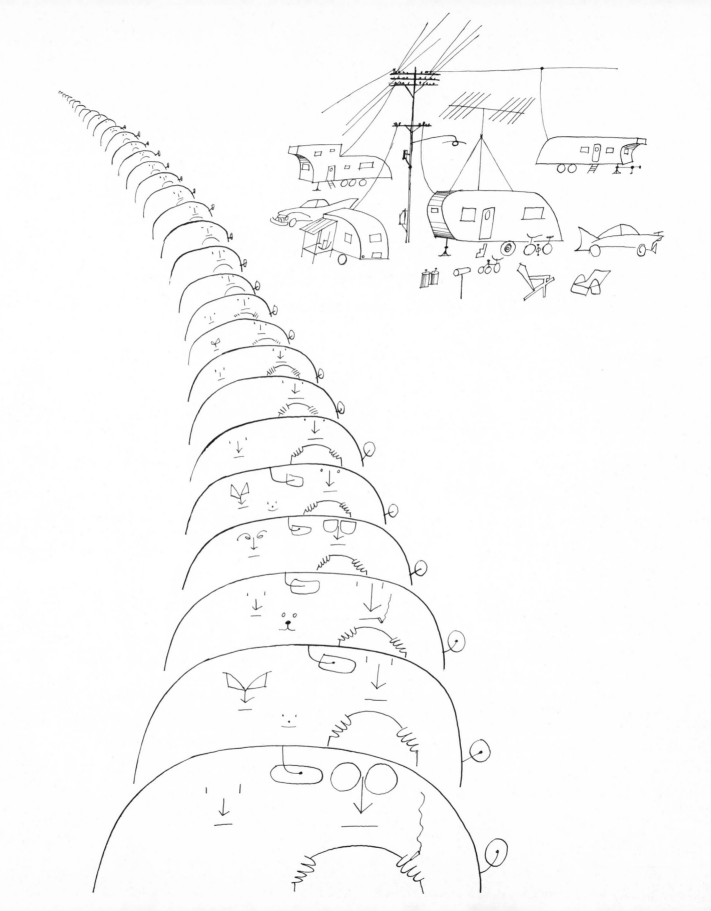

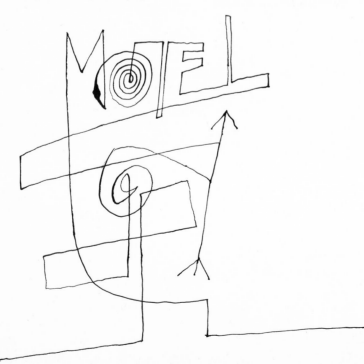

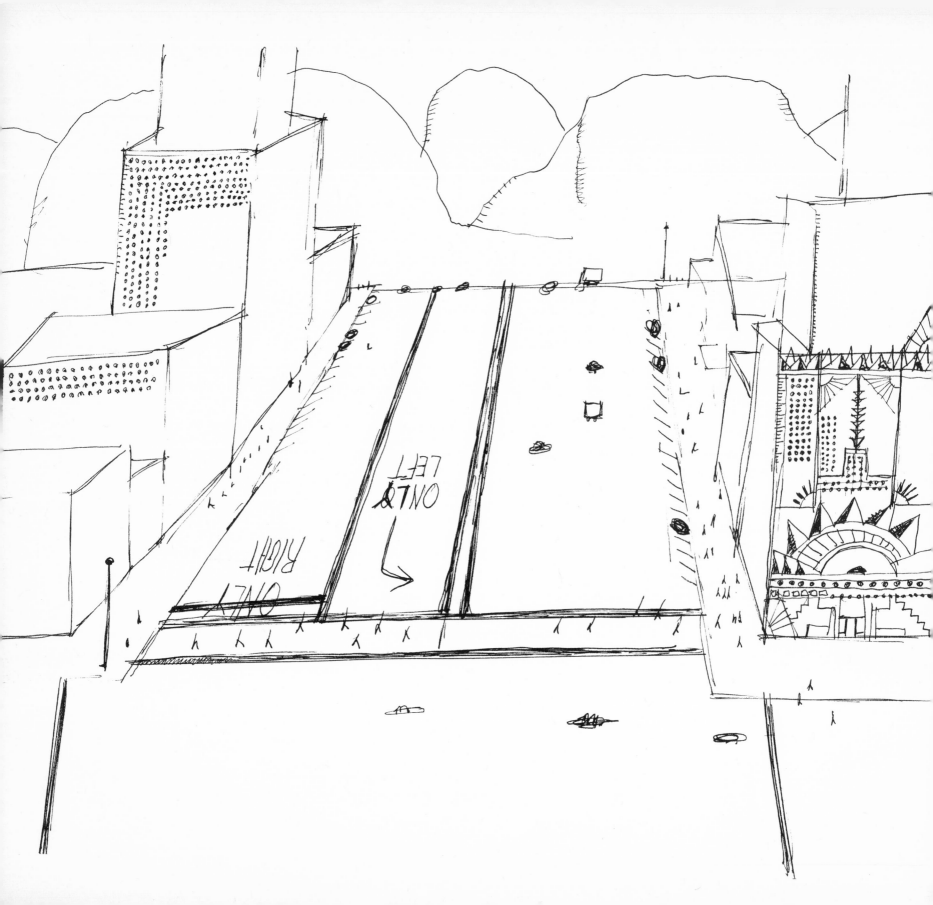

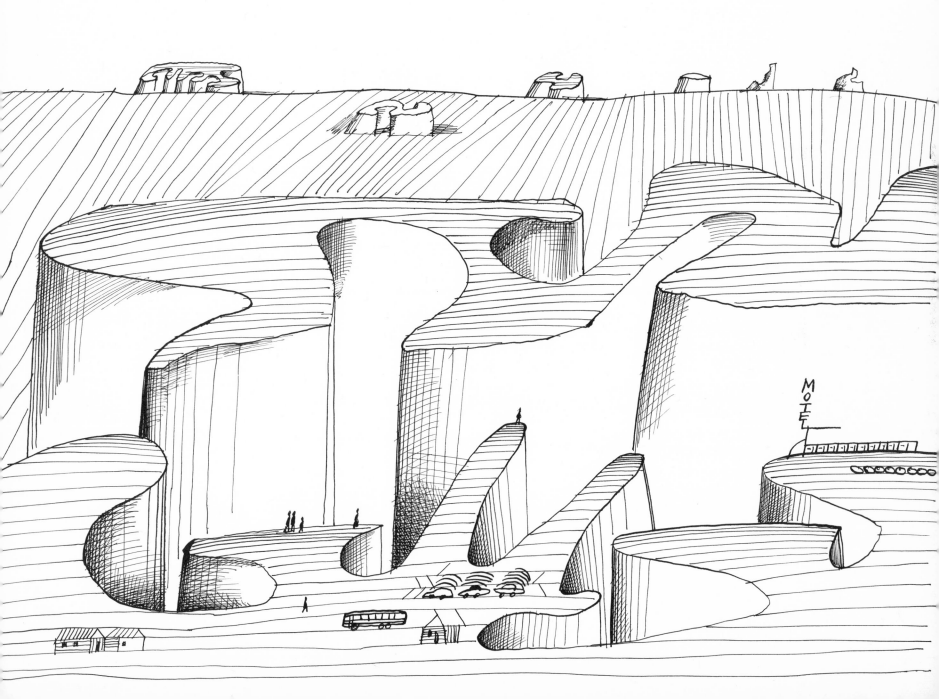

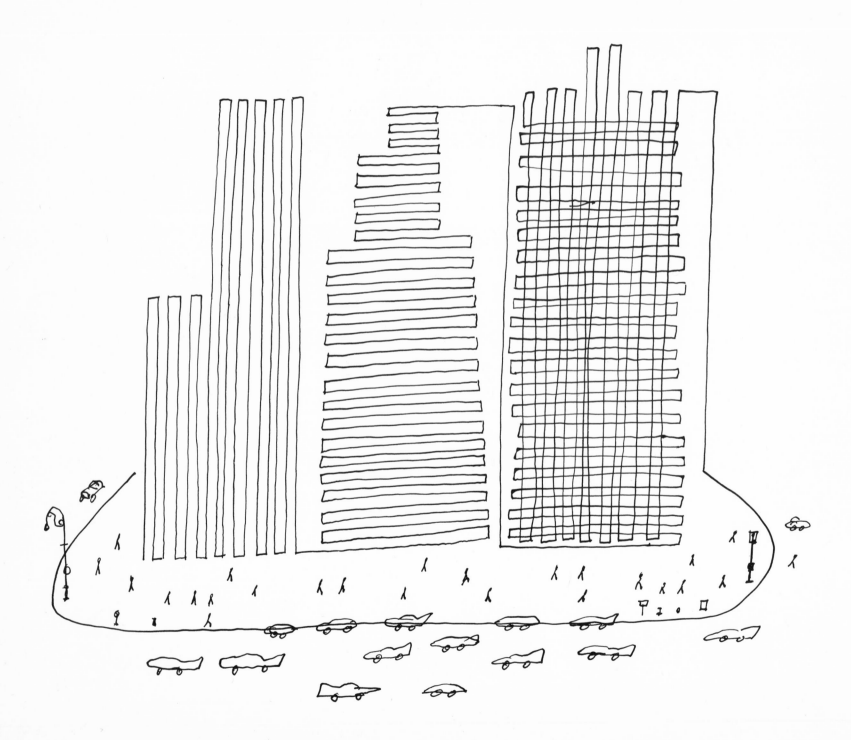

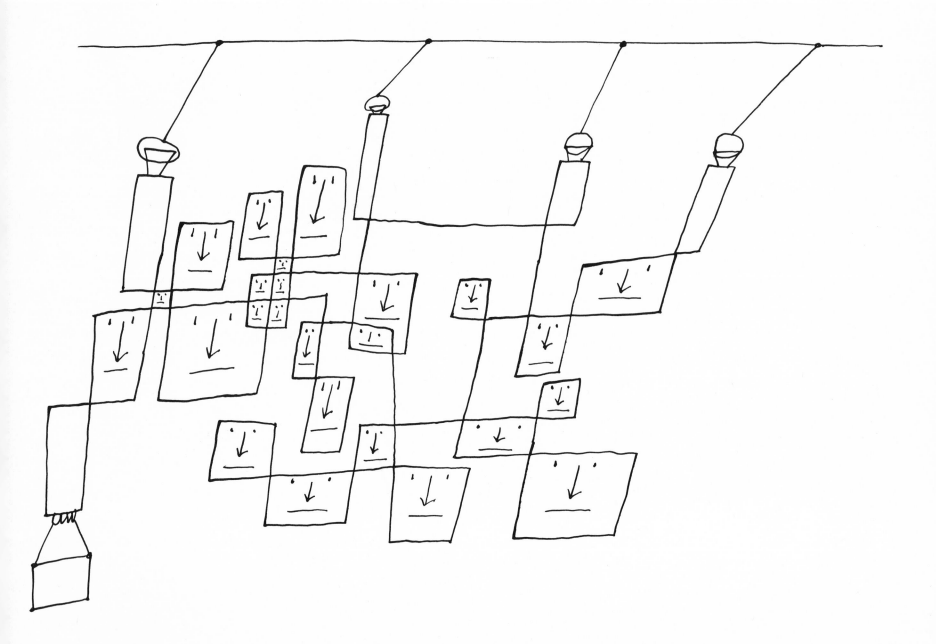

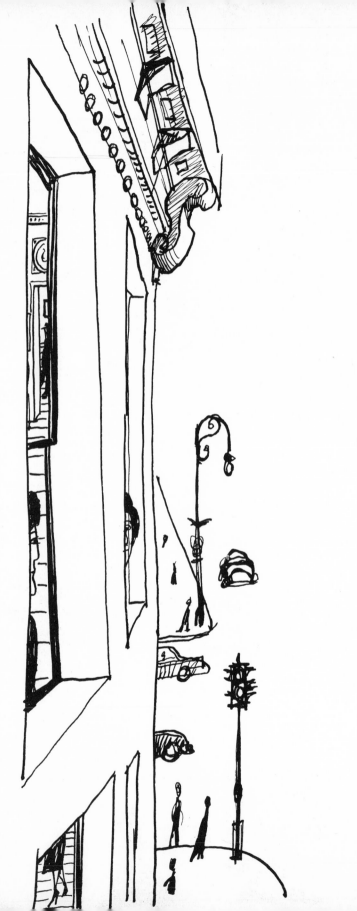

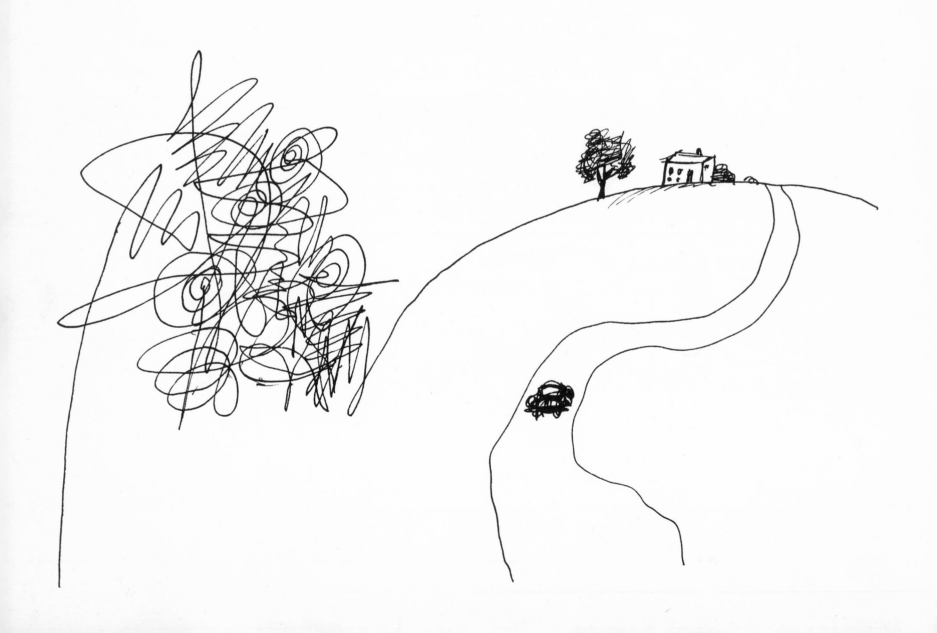

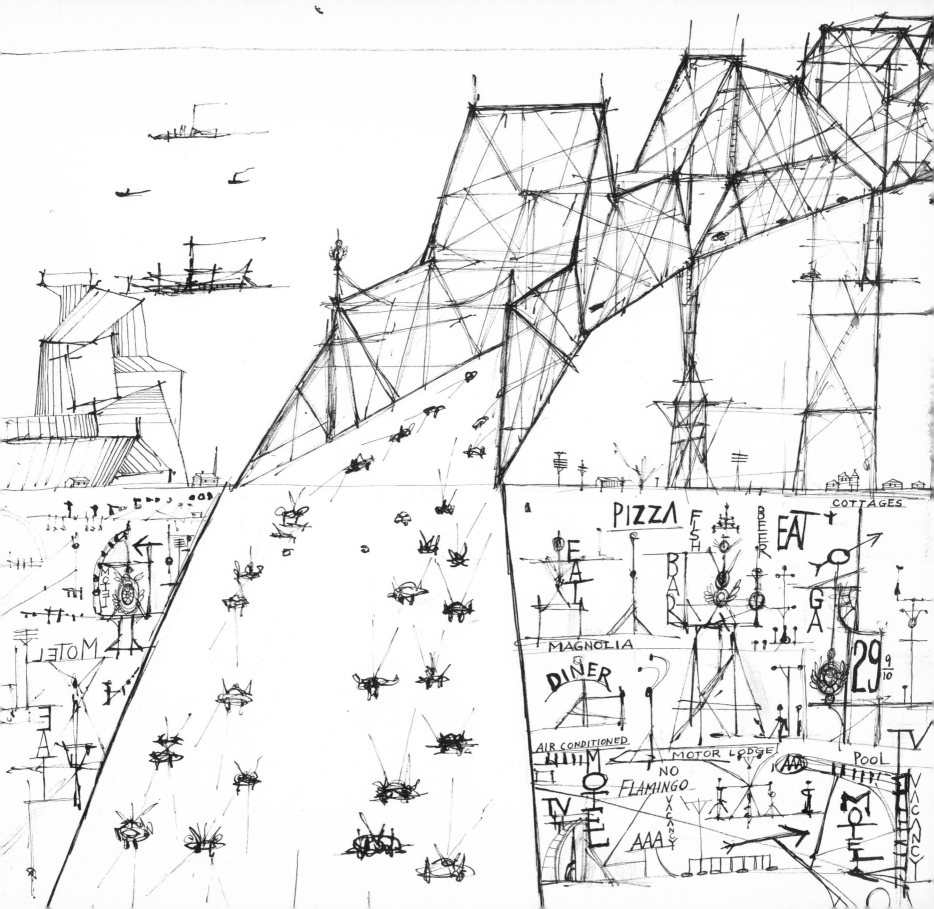

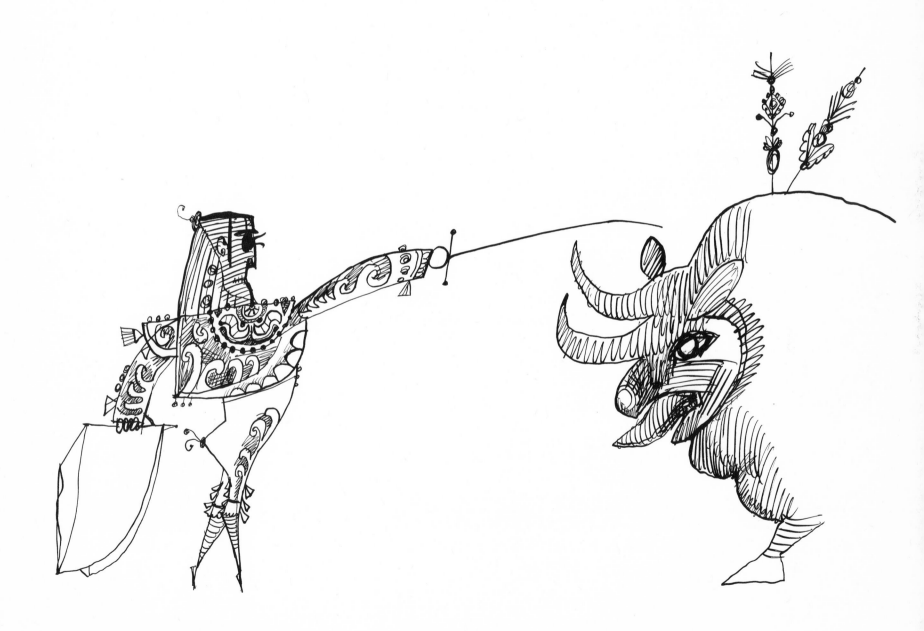

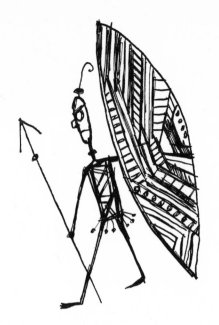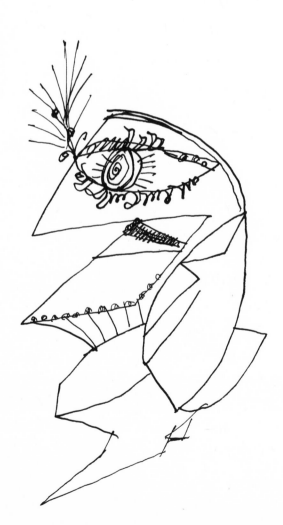

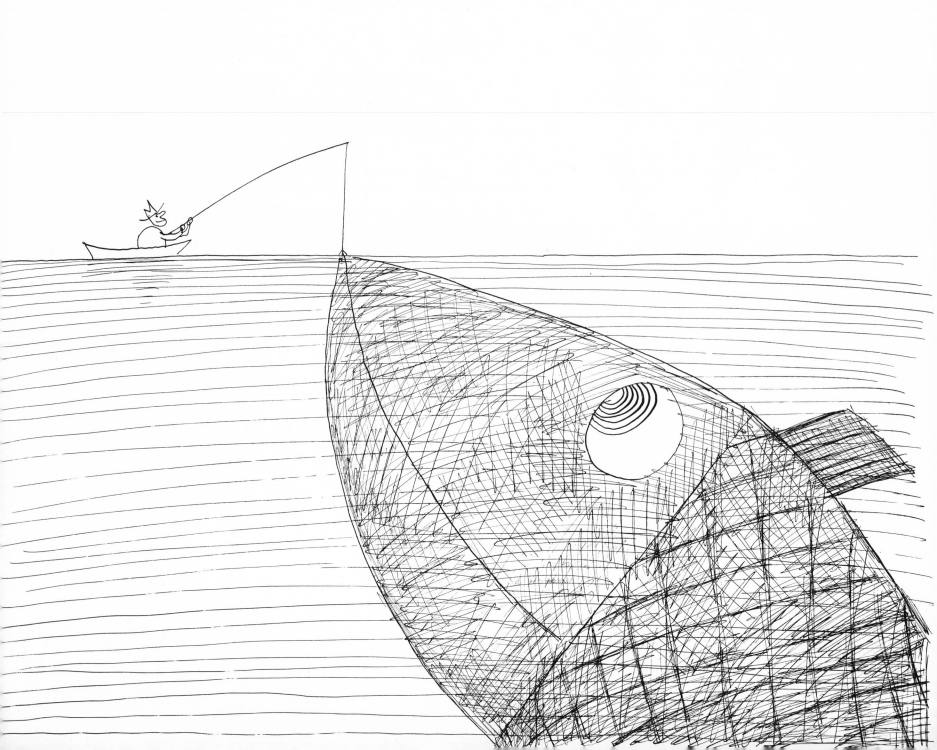

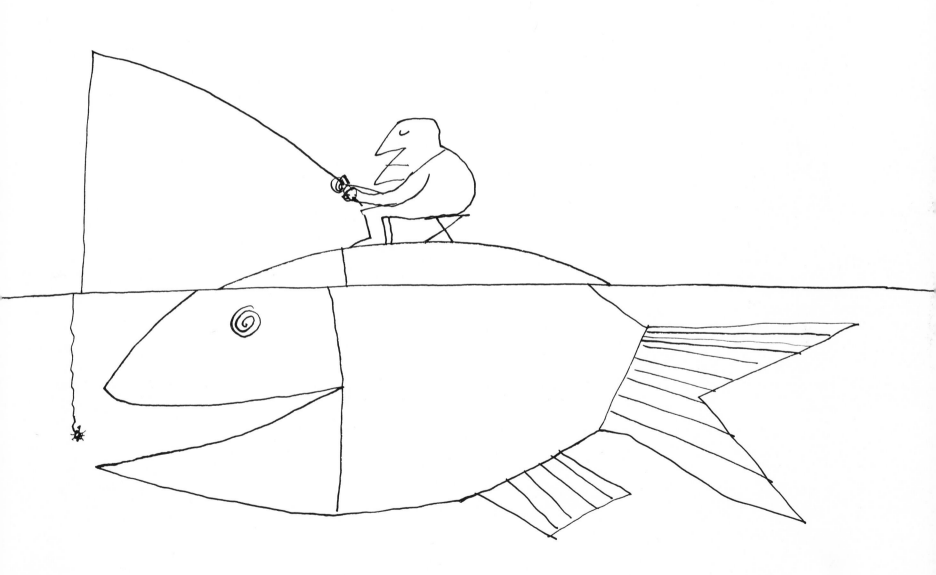

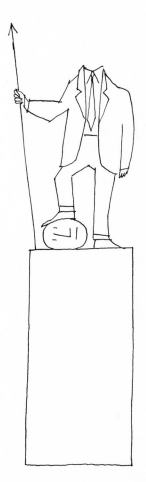

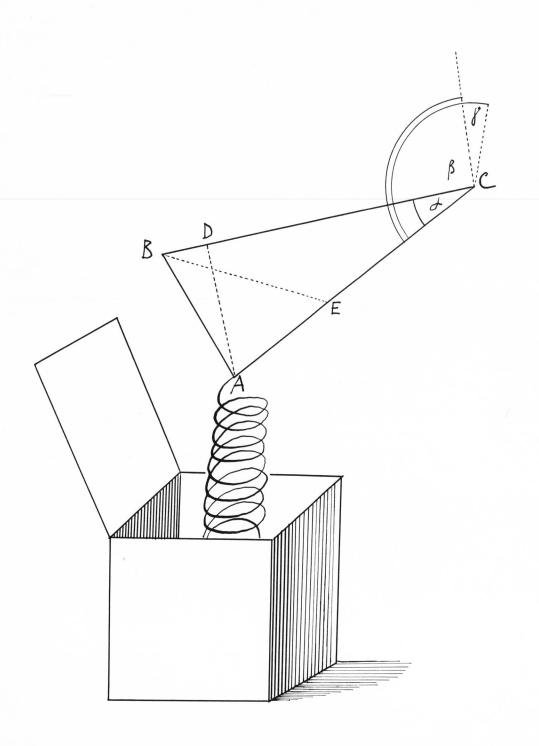

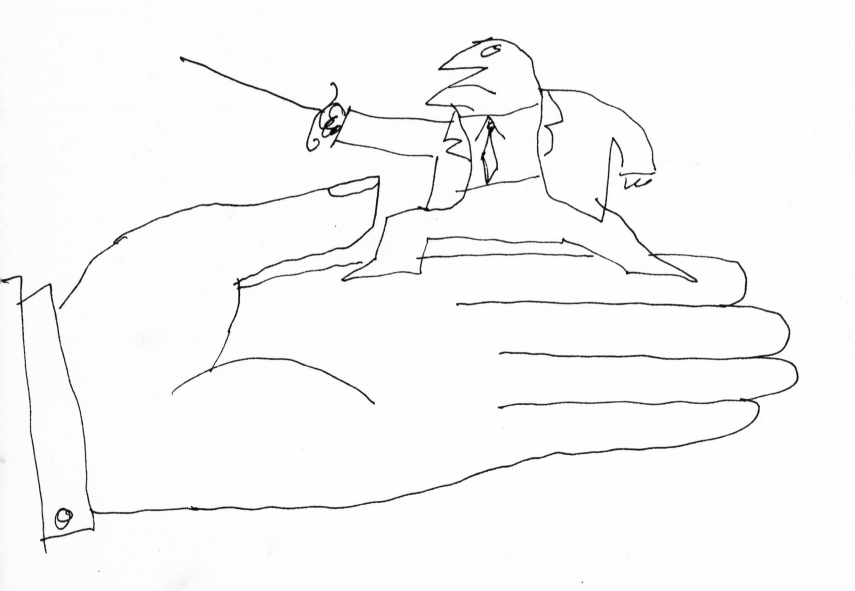

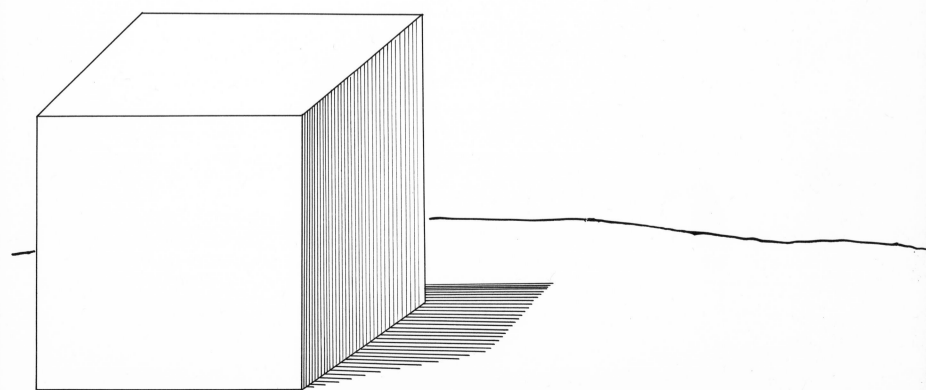

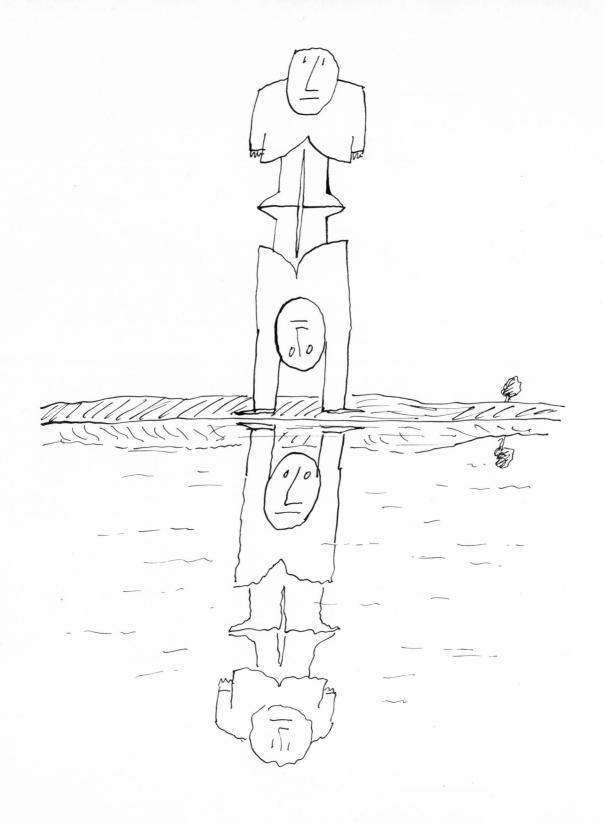

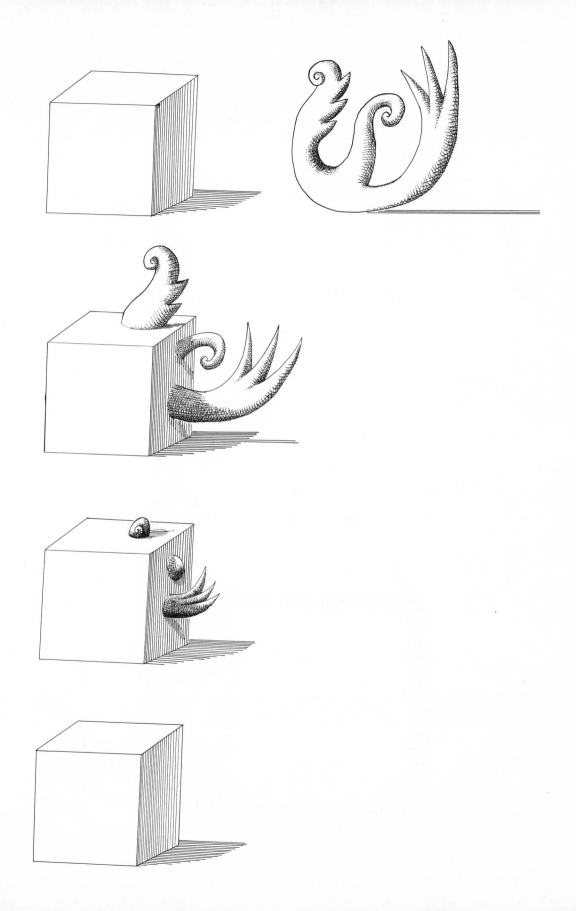

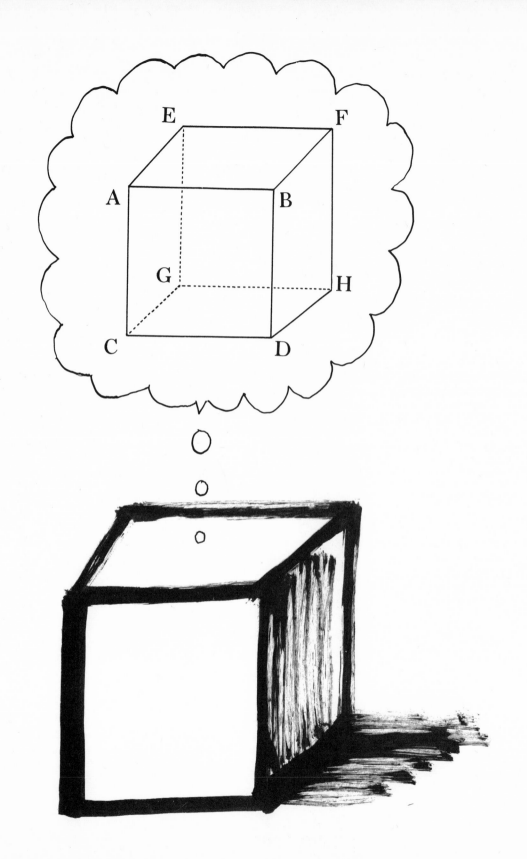

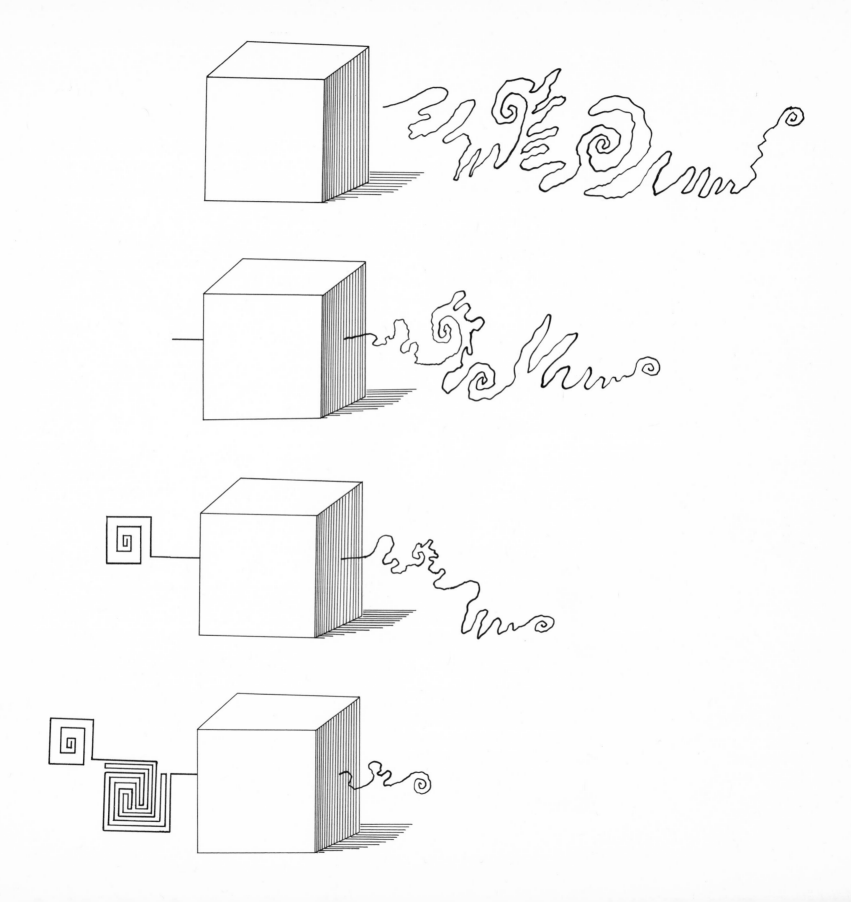

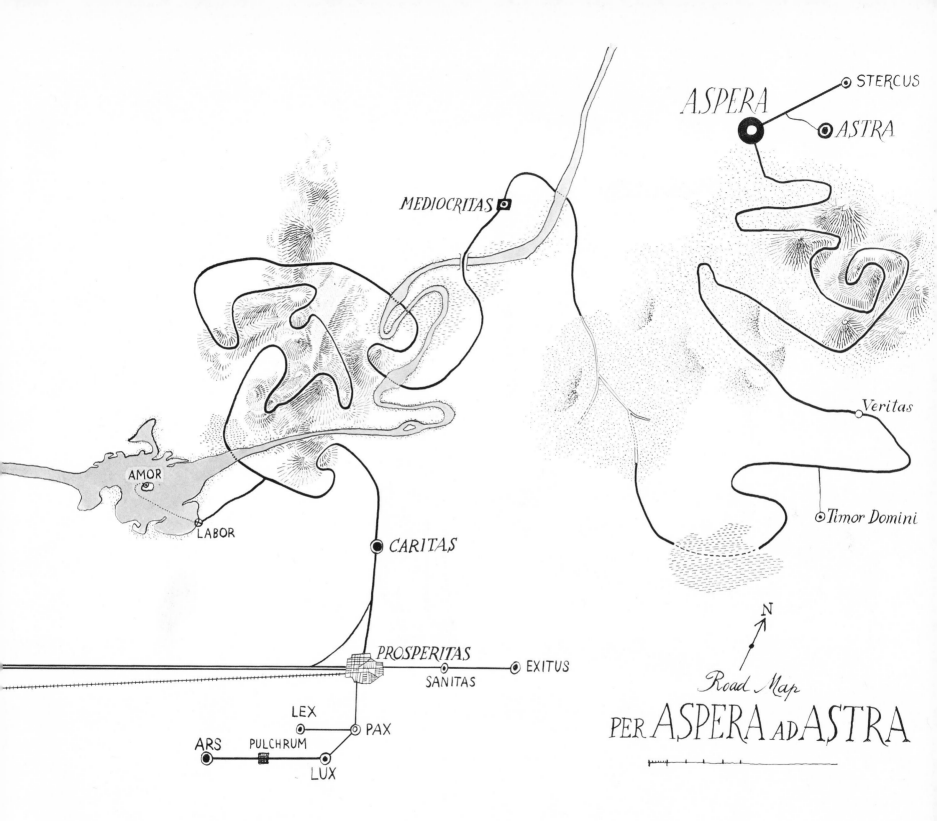

STERCUS

ASPERA

ASTRA

MEDIOCRITAS

Veritas

Timor Domini

AMOR

LABOR

CARITAS

PROSPERITAS

SANITAS

EXITUS

LEX

PAX

ARS

PULCHRUM

LUX

N

Road Map

PER ASPERA AD ASTRA

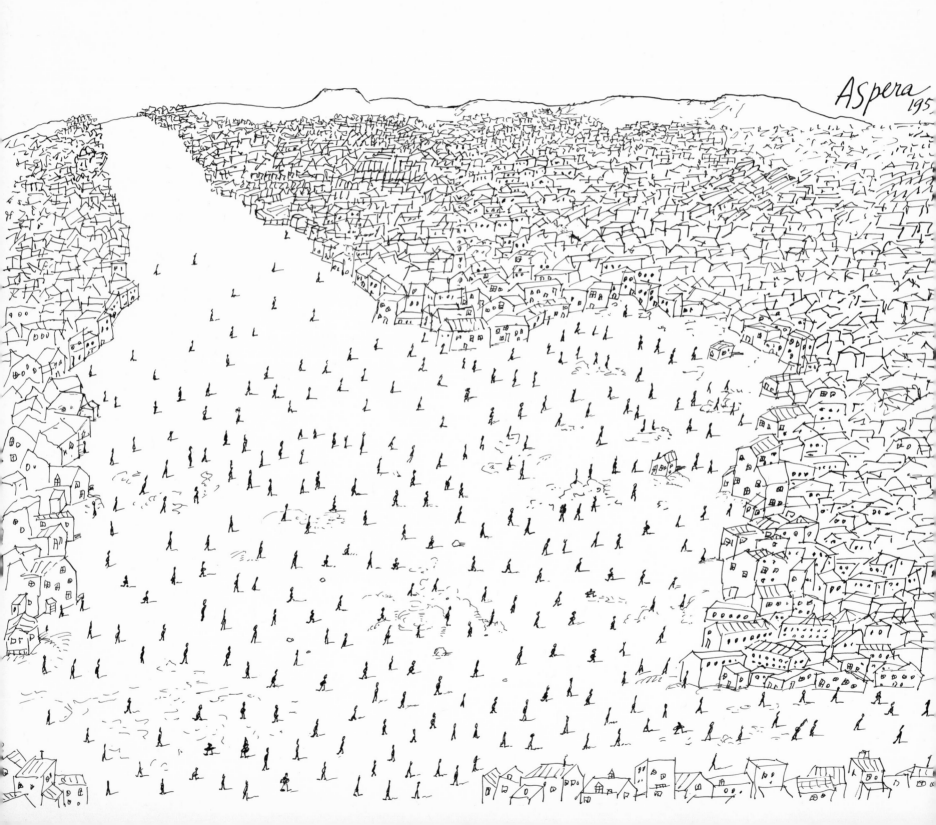

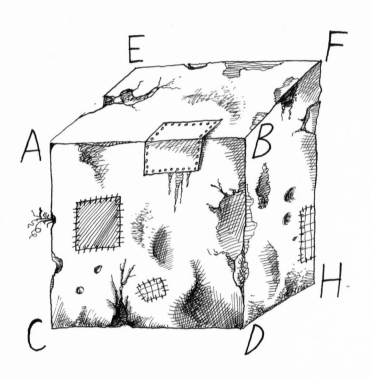

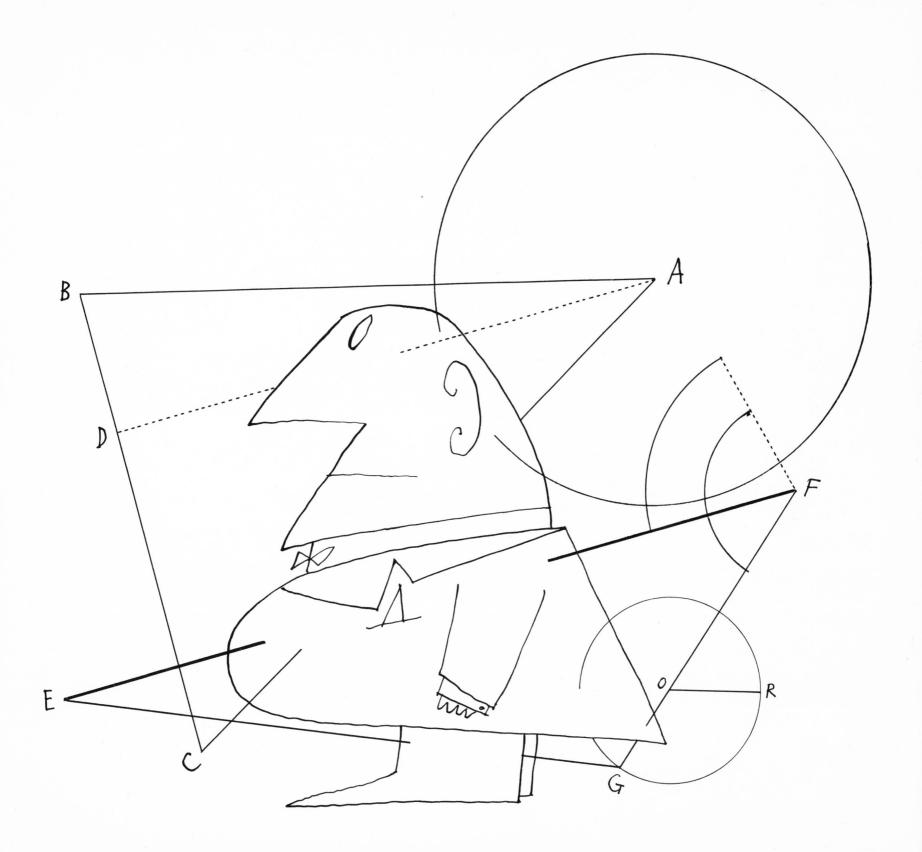

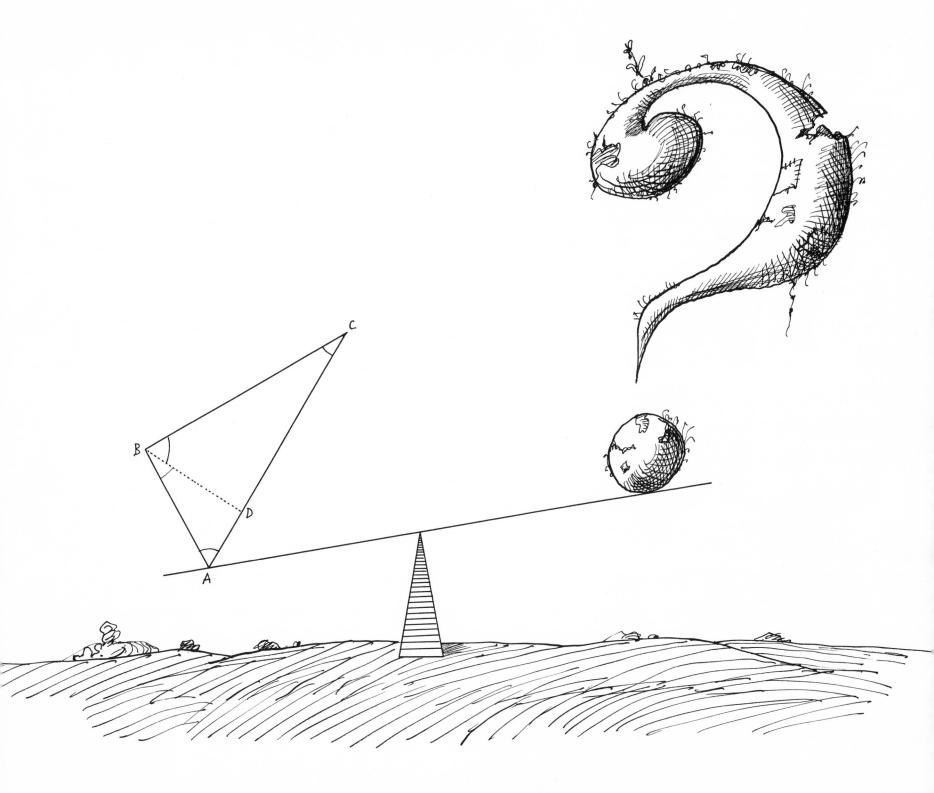

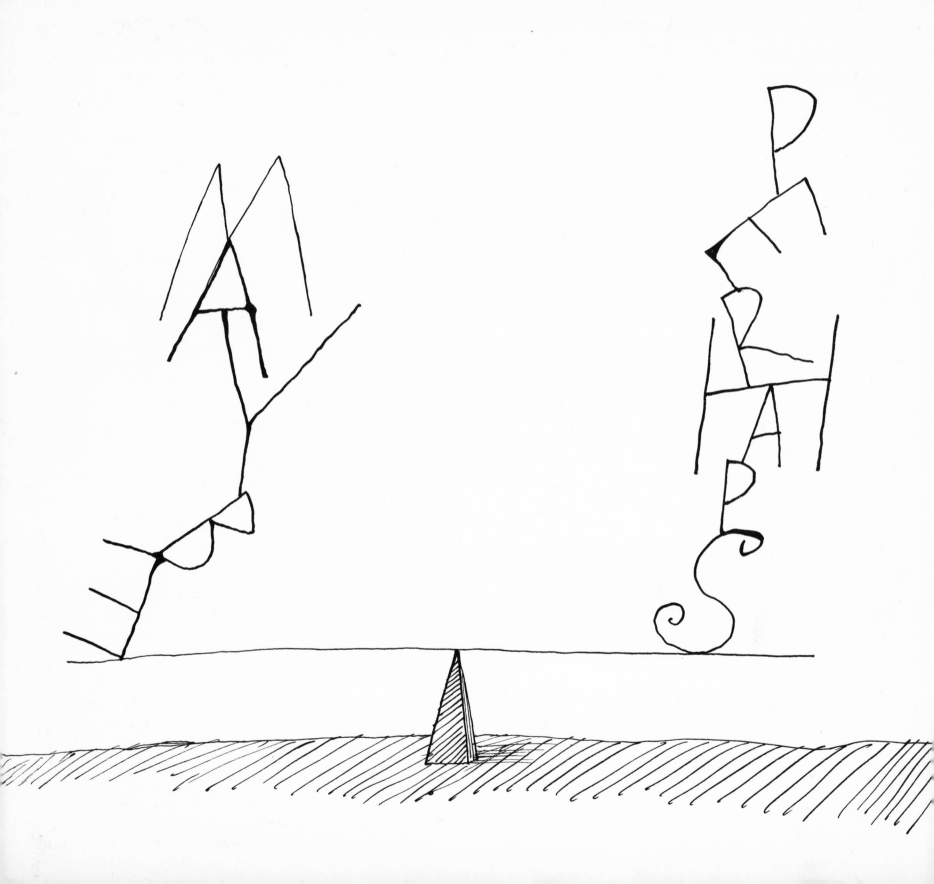

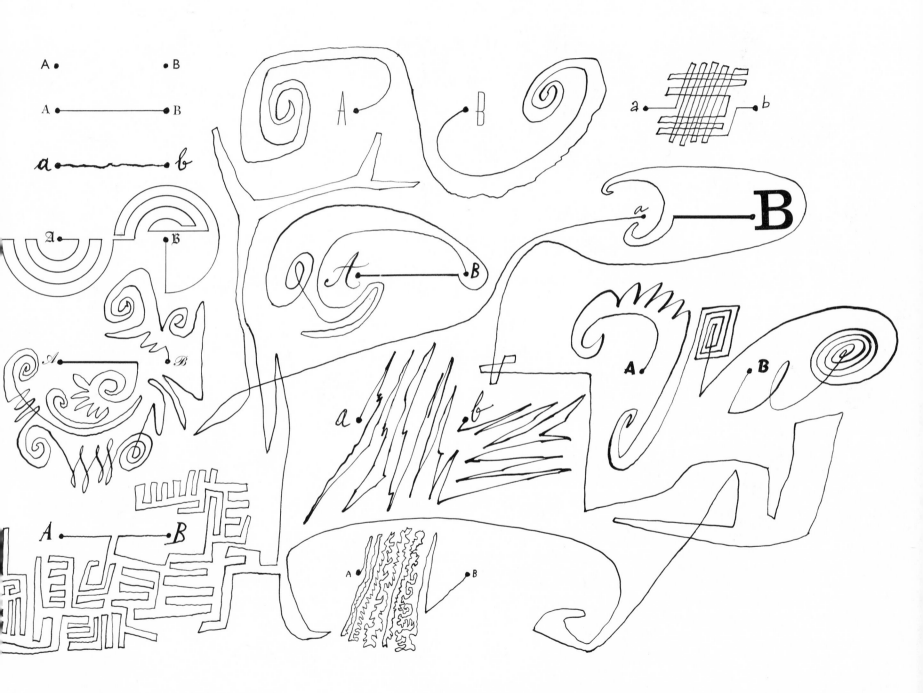